STAR WARS™

X-WING

STAR WARS™
X-WING

WRITTEN BY MICHAEL KOGGE

INCREDI
BUILDS

A Division of Insight Editions, LP
San Rafael, California

INTRODUCTION

In its fight against the evil Empire, the Rebel Alliance was always vastly outnumbered. It couldn't call on fleets of Star Destroyers to lead attacks. Nor could it deploy squadrons upon squadrons of TIE fighters without concern over losses. Despite this colossal imbalance, the Alliance did possess one asset the Empire lacked: a special weapon that destroyed thousands of TIEs, crippled more than a few Star Destroyers, and even atomized two Death Stars.

The rebels had the X-wing—a vehicle so versatile and deadly that many Alliance leaders readily admit that without it, the Empire would have crushed the Rebellion once and for all. Perhaps the greatest testament to the X-wing's success is its longevity. Decades after its introduction, the X-wing remains in service for the forces of the New Republic and the Resistance.

This one-man starfighter boasts a design as utilitarian as it is elegant. Its tapered nose expands into a long, narrow fuselage that encompasses a cockpit and droid slot before terminating in four S-foil wings, each equipped with laser cannons and powerful engines. To increase its firing range during combat runs, these S-foils open up in a crisscross pattern that gives the X-wing its name. Deflector shields and durasteel plating protect the fighter from enemy fire, while hyperspace motivators in each engine unit allow it to quickly enter or escape the field of battle. Moreover, the socketed astromech droid can perform repairs, compute astronavigational coordinates, and even operate the ship if necessary, giving X-wing pilots an edge over TIE fighter pilots, who lack such support.

Though it may not achieve the extreme speeds of the A-wing or carry the heavy ordnance of the Y-wing, the X-wing compensates by filling the middle ground between these two sister craft by being both fast and well armed, making it the ultimate, all-purpose starfighter. With a good pilot at its controls, the X-wing can tangle with TIE fighters as effectively as an A-wing or run a bombing campaign in place of a Y-wing. The Rebel Alliance, New Republic, and Resistance have all depended on this versatility to accomplish the most daring of missions, from long–distance reconnaissance to outflanking Imperial armadas.

T-65 X-WING

The original T-65 X-wing was the jack-of-all-trades in the Rebellion's starfighter fleet. Rugged yet agile and able to deliver quite a punch, it proved to be the sharpest thorn in the Imperial Navy's side.

TECHNICAL SPECIFICATIONS

MANUFACTURER: Incom Corporation

MODEL: T-65 X-wing

CLASS: Starfighter

WIDTH/HEIGHT/DEPTH:
11.46 m x 3.08 m x 13.31 m

WEAPONRY: Four laser cannons; two proton torpedo launchers

SHIELDS: Yes

MAXIMUM SPEED: 3,700 G (space) / 1,050 kph (atmosphere)

HYPERDRIVE: Class 1

LIFE SUPPORT SYSTEMS: Yes

CREW: 1 + astromech droid

CONSUMABLES: One-week supply

COST: 150,000 Imperial credits new; 90,000 used (military requisition charges)

INCOM GBK-585 HYPER-DRIVE MOTIVATOR (4): Built into the engine nacelles, all four form a hyperspace jump initiation circuit, equivalent to a hyperdrive with a Class 1 multiplier.

INCOM 4L4 FUSIAL THRUST ENGINES: Power converters, alluvial dampeners, turbo impellers, and lateral stabilizers make these some of the most efficient engines ever designed.

S-FOIL WINGS: Wings close for long-distance travel and unlatch in combat situations.

CARGO COMPARTMENT: A two-cubic-meter hold offers pilots a place to stash survival gear or special equipment for extended missions.

KRUPX MG7 PROTON TORPEDO LAUNCHER (2): Each launcher is loaded with a magazine of three torpedoes.

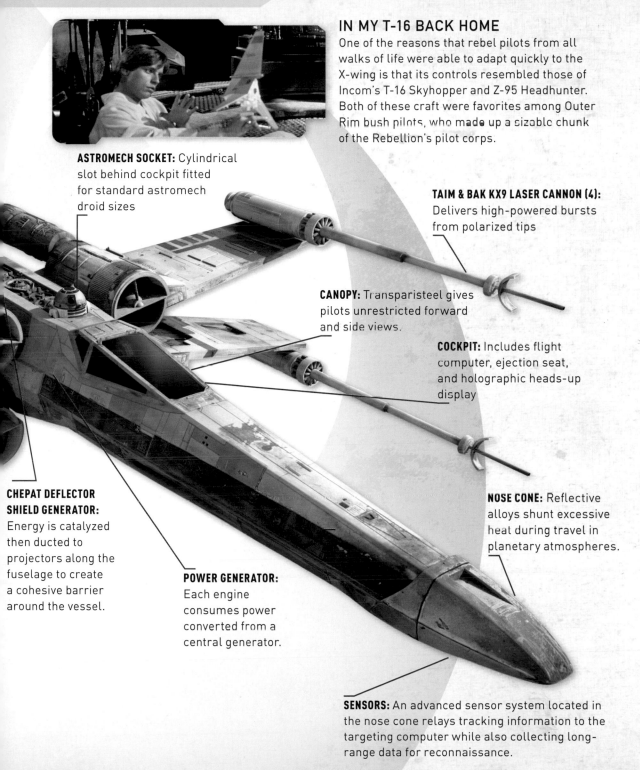

IN MY T-16 BACK HOME

One of the reasons that rebel pilots from all walks of life were able to adapt quickly to the X-wing is that its controls resembled those of Incom's T-16 Skyhopper and Z-95 Headhunter. Both of these craft were favorites among Outer Rim bush pilots, who made up a sizable chunk of the Rebellion's pilot corps.

ASTROMECH SOCKET: Cylindrical slot behind cockpit fitted for standard astromech droid sizes

TAIM & BAK KX9 LASER CANNON (4): Delivers high-powered bursts from polarized tips

CANOPY: Transparisteel gives pilots unrestricted forward and side views.

COCKPIT: Includes flight computer, ejection seat, and holographic heads-up display

CHEPAT DEFLECTOR SHIELD GENERATOR: Energy is catalyzed then ducted to projectors along the fuselage to create a cohesive barrier around the vessel.

POWER GENERATOR: Each engine consumes power converted from a central generator.

NOSE CONE: Reflective alloys shunt excessive heat during travel in planetary atmospheres.

SENSORS: An advanced sensor system located in the nose cone relays tracking information to the targeting computer while also collecting long-range data for reconnaissance.

FIERCE FIGHTER

The Empire and First Order learned the hard way not to underestimate the X-wing's capabilities. An X-wing may be slower and less maneuverable than a TIE, but its many other attributes—particularly its combat capability—make it the superior starfighter.

ARMED TO THE NOSE

The X-wing has double the laser weaponry found in a basic TIE, as each wing is armed with a long-barrel KX9 cannon. Pilots can unleash all four cannons at once, trigger individual cannons for precision shots, or fire any desired combination to maintain a constant barrage. Parabolic dishes around each polarized tip suppress possible "flashback" of excess energy that could melt the cannon.

PROTON PACKER

If laser cannons prove inadequate, an X-wing's proton torpedos can finish the job. When the target is properly locked, these energy missiles are able to pierce ray shields and inflict damage on a scale that few TIEs—and even moon-sized battle stations—can weather!

QUALITY VS. QUANTITY

The number of X-wings the rebels built during the Galactic Civil War paled compared to the hundreds of thousands of TIEs that Sienar Fleet Systems pumped out for the Empire. Nonetheless, because of Incom's engineers' insistence on using state-of-the-art componentry and hand-assembly techniques, the X-wing proved superior to the mass-produced Empire fighters. Constructing an X-wing cost more than double the price to construct a TIE, but its battle-survival rate was many times higher.

LOCK AND LOAD

When an X-wing enters a combat zone, two wings seemingly become four. Servos split the starfighter's S-foils to offer the pilot an expanded field of fire for its laser cannons. For faster travel, particularly in atmosphere and hyperspace, the S-foils collapse to reduce drag.

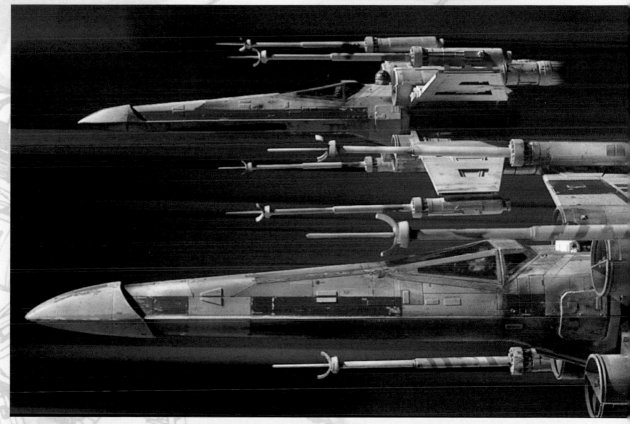

TOUGH TARGET

The X-wing's narrow shape makes it hard for enemy gunners to acquire a lock on it. Even then, a direct hit might fizzle against the X-wing's deflector shields or be absorbed by its reinforced titanium hull. Often TIE fighter pilots mistakenly believe they've downed their enemy only to have the X-wing withstand the TIE attack and respond with a barrage of its own.

AIM AID

The sensor array at the X-wing's nose pings the location of surrounding craft and transmits this information to the tracking computer and astro-mech droid. In conjunction, these machines calculate all available firing windows for the cockpit's heads-up display, where a simple three-dimensional wireframe view eschews visual distractions to focus on what's essential: the target.

RECON ROGUE

Space duels with TIE fighters are only one arena where the X-wing shines. It also serves as the ideal craft for reconnaissance, espionage, and rescue missions. Those who have the privilege of flying an X-wing must be able to leave the cockpit and perform daring ground operations that no TIE fighter pilot would ever be asked to do.

PETULANT PARTNER

Flesh-and-blood X-wing pilots are not alone in their endeavors. Plugged in behind every pilot is a robotic right hand—an astromech unit that monitors all the ship's instrumentation to ensure top performance. The droid can perform complicated navigation computations, execute repairs during combat, and even fly the X-wing if the pilot becomes incapacitated or just needs to rest on long journeys. Many pilots become attached to their assigned droids and refrain from wiping their memory banks, concerned that the droid might lose its special connection to them. Consequently, these astromechs can develop quirky personalities of their own and often become as cocky and brash as the pilots!

QUICK GETAWAYS

Unlike all standard TIE models, the X-wing is outfitted with the biggest lifesaver of all: a hyperdrive. The Class 1 unit permits travel to distant locales without the aid of a hyperdrive booster ring or being ferried by a capital ship. It also gives pilots the option to duck out of hopeless battles and live to fight another day.

SOLO SCOUT

The sensor system on the X-wing can be set for silent-passive or high-transmission-active mode, with the ability to scan wide or specify signatures and areas to narrow the search. The array at the nose of the craft gathers its data through a Carbanti universal transceiver that contains components for full-spectrum lock tracking, energy multi-imaging, and low-level terrain discernment. Both the Fabritech ANq sensor computers and astromech droid analyze the data and provide the pilot with their interpretations. Lone X-wing pilots are often tasked with jumping into enemy territory, collecting data about military targets, and jumping out before being noticed.

JAMMIN' AWAY

Sometimes the X-wing's most valuable defense isn't its deflector shields or hull, but the Betriak "Screamer" system that many craft possess. It creates noise on the electromagnetic spectrum that can confuse the tracking systems of TIE fighters or seeker missiles.

T-70 X-WING

The T-70 X-wing adheres to the old engineering axiom that "if it ain't broke, don't fix it." Built decades after the T-65, it retains much of its predecessor's classic design, with some minor enhancements that ensure it remains the superior starfighter in the galaxy.

TECHNICAL SPECIFICATIONS

MANUFACTURER: Incom Corporation

MODEL: T-70 X-wing

CLASS: Starfighter

WIDTH/HEIGHT/DEPTH: 12.49 m x 11.26 m x 2.73 m

WEAPONRY: Four laser cannons; two proton torpedo launchers

SHIELDS: Yes

MAXIMUM SPEED: 3,800 G (space) / 1,100 kph (atmosphere)

HYPERDRIVE: Class 1

LIFE SUPPORT SYSTEMS: Yes

CREW: 1 + astromech droid

CONSUMABLES: One-week supply

COST: 210,000 Republic credits new; 120,000 used (military requisition charges)

BLACK ONE
Resistance pilot Poe Dameron's customized T-70 X-wing sports a black ferrosphere paint coat that scatters the pings of enemy sensors, making it harder to hit.

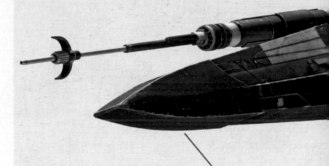

SENSORS: An advanced linked system throughout the cone relays tracking information to the targeting computer while also permitting long-range data collection for reconnaissance.

SCARCE STARFIGHTERS
The Resistance finds itself in the same conundrum as the former Rebel Alliance in acquiring an ample supply of X-wings. New Republic demilitarization policies, along with starship trade monopolies, have forced the Resistance to rely on wealthy donors sympathetic to its cause to maintain its small starfighter corps.

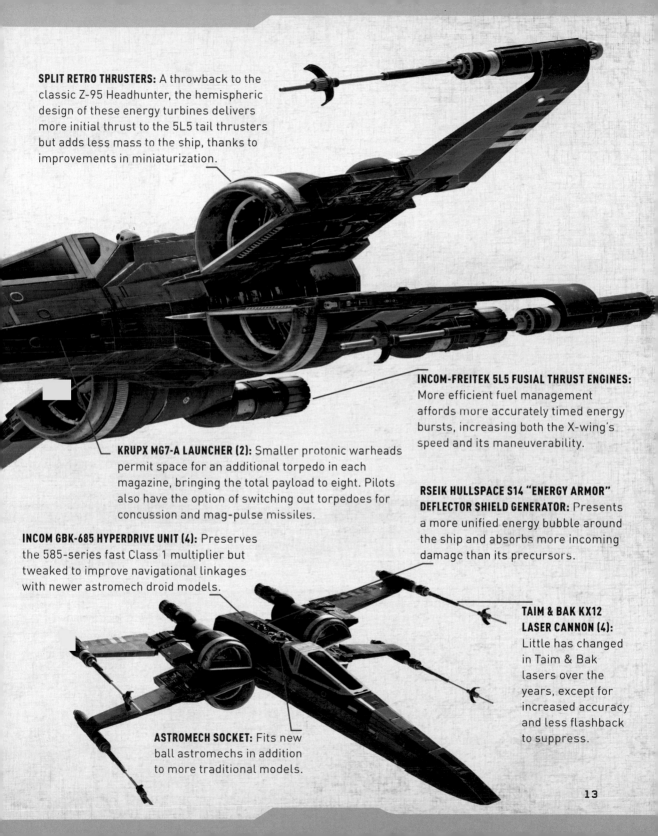

SPLIT RETRO THRUSTERS: A throwback to the classic Z-95 Headhunter, the hemispheric design of these energy turbines delivers more initial thrust to the 5L5 tail thrusters but adds less mass to the ship, thanks to improvements in miniaturization.

INCOM-FREITEK 5L5 FUSIAL THRUST ENGINES: More efficient fuel management affords more accurately timed energy bursts, increasing both the X-wing's speed and its maneuverability.

KRUPX MG7-A LAUNCHER (2): Smaller protonic warheads permit space for an additional torpedo in each magazine, bringing the total payload to eight. Pilots also have the option of switching out torpedoes for concussion and mag-pulse missiles.

RSEIK HULLSPACE S14 "ENERGY ARMOR" DEFLECTOR SHIELD GENERATOR: Presents a more unified energy bubble around the ship and absorbs more incoming damage than its precursors.

INCOM GBK-685 HYPERDRIVE UNIT (4): Preserves the 585-series fast Class 1 multiplier but tweaked to improve navigational linkages with newer astromech droid models.

TAIM & BAK KX12 LASER CANNON (4): Little has changed in Taim & Bak lasers over the years, except for increased accuracy and less flashback to suppress.

ASTROMECH SOCKET: Fits new ball astromechs in addition to more traditional models.

13

BIG SHOTS

Though many have flown in the cockpit of an X-wing, two pilots stand out in the course of galactic history: Luke Skywalker and Poe Dameron.

LUKE SKYWALKER, REBEL PILOT

Luke spent his teenage years racing T-16 Skyhoppers through Beggar's Canyon on Tatooine, so he had little trouble grasping the X-wing's controls or flying down the trench of the Death Star.

One in a Million

To the consternation of the Rebel Alliance leaders, Luke Skywalker switched off his X-wing's targeting computer while aiming at the Death Star's reactor. He relied instead on his own marksmanship, combined with a latent talent in the Force, to fire proton torpedoes down the reactor shaft. His incredible shot found its mark, initiating a chain reaction that destroyed the Death Star and gave hope to champions of freedom across the galaxy.

Jedi Jet

As his father did before him, Luke Skywalker flew a starfighter to complete his Jedi missions. The T-65B X-wing proved a perfect vessel for Luke and his astromech companion, R2-D2; it was fast, tough, and could get them wherever they needed to go with its hyperdrive. Of all the obstacles in the galaxy, the only thing that nearly grounded it for good were the bogs of Dagobah.

POE DAMERON, RESISTANCE PILOT

Poe grew up the son of Shara Bey, an A-wing pilot who fought in the Battle of Endor, so he had a jump start from an early age in learning how to fly starfighters.

Lost Ship

During Poe's mission to retrieve an important artifact on Jakku, the First Order destroyed his X-wing and took Poe prisoner aboard its Star Destroyer. Since the Resistance possessed very few starfighters, the loss of even one was costly. Fortunately, Poe escaped the Star Destroyer in a TIE fighter and was able to jump back into a T-70 cockpit to help turn the tide against the First Order at Takodana.

Ace Command

For starfighter engagements in which secrecy isn't mandated, Poe flies a customized black T-70 with orange racing stripes known as *Black One*. He captained both Red and Blue Squadrons as "Black Leader" in the battles of Takodana and Starkiller Base, where his high-flying skills and expert leadership saved many pilots' lives and contributed to the Resistance's biggest victory— the destruction of the Starkiller superweapon.

PILOTS OF THE REBELLION

Countless men and women dedicated their lives as Rebel Alliance X-wing pilots to liberate the galaxy from the shackles of the Empire.

BIGGS DARKLIGHTER

Biggs and his best friend, Luke Skywalker, both dreamed of entering the Imperial Academy to train as pilots, but only Darklighter left Tatooine to do so. His time as an Imperial was short-lived, and not long after graduation he defected to the Rebellion. His path crossed with Skywalker's for a final time at the Battle of Yavin, during which the two flew as wingmates. Darklighter perished in the Death Star trenches under Darth Vader's lasers, but his sacrifice allowed Skywalker to trigger the shot that destroyed the Death Star.

WEDGE ANTILLES

One of the few surviving Rebel pilots at the Battle of Yavin, Wedge went on to have a stellar career for the Rebellion and New Republic. He flew a snowspeeder for Rogue Group during the Imperial assault on Hoth to help his rebel comrades evacuate their base. At the Battle of Endor, he commanded Red Squadron and led the charge alongside the *Millennium Falcon* into the Death Star's superstructure.

JEK PORKINS

Porkins had a storied flight record, having accomplished many missions for the Rebellion. Sadly, "Red Six" was one of the first X-wing pilots lost at the Battle of Yavin. The memory of him, however, continued to burn bright in the hearts of rebels for years afterward.

PILOTS OF THE RESISTANCE

A new generation of X-wing pilots fights for the Resistance against the oppressive First Order.

JESSIKA PAVA

Youth is not a limiting factor for Pava; she puts many of the older, more experienced Resistance pilots to shame. When flying X-wings, she's "Blue Three" of Blue Squadron, though on the ground her friends just call her "Jess" or "Testor."

NIEN NUNB

Famed for copiloting the *Millennium Falcon* with Lando Calrissian at the Battle of Endor, Nien Nunb refused to retire from the cockpit, especially when tyranny was on the march yet again. The Resistance was overjoyed to have in their ranks this brave Sullustan, who's capable of flying just about anything with an engine.

TEMMIN "SNAP" WEXLEY

Born on Akiva to parents who had ties to the Rebellion, Wexley later followed in their footsteps and joined the Resistance. His reconnaissance flight targeting Starkiller Base provided the Resistance with the intelligence necessary to formulate an attack to destroy it. Captain Wexley gladly participated in that attack as a member of Blue Squadron under Poe Dameron's command.

X-WING BATTLES

During the war against the Galactic Empire, rebel X-wing pilots braved overwhelming odds to help put an end to tyranny. With the First Order on the rise, the Resistance now continues the fight one battle at a time.

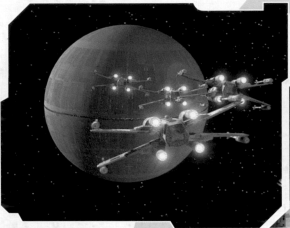 

BATTLE OF YAVIN

When the Death Star threatened to obliterate the Rebel Alliance's hidden base on Yavin 4, just thirty starfighters were mobilized to protect the planet. Grand Moff Tarkin, the battle station's overseer, deemed the rebels' response trivial, and did not bother to launch TIE squadrons to intercept the X-wings. Only Darth Vader acknowledged the danger the rebels posed, and if not for one X-wing pilot gifted in the Force, Vader and his TIE squadron would have driven off the rebels, and Yavin 4 would have met the same fiery fate as Alderaan.

BATTLE OF ENDOR

Admiral Ackbar's daring plan was to bring the entire Rebel Alliance fleet to Endor in a surprise attack on the Emperor's second Death Star. The rebels sent just about every X-wing they possessed into a war zone thick with TIE fighters and Star Destroyers. Many gave their lives just to buy time for the rebel commandos on the forest moon who were trying to destroy the Death Star's shield generator. When the shields came down, a couple of X-wings accompanied the *Millennium Falcon* through the labyrinth of the Death Star's superstructure and helped detonate the power core. It proved the turning point in toppling the Galactic Empire.

BATTLE OF TAKODANA

Alerted that BB-8 was in Maz Kanata's castle on Takodana, the Resistance sent a small force to rescue the ball-shaped droid and the vital information he carried. A squadron of T-70 X-wings led the attack, plummeting through the atmosphere and skimming over the opalescent surface of Takodana's lakes. They found the First Order had already beaten them to the planet and had leveled the castle to smoking ruins. When the X-wings arrived, the First Order quickly turned tail and retreated to space, taking with it not BB-8 but another prisoner: a tech scavenger from Jakku named Rey.

BATTLE OF STARKILLER BASE

After annihilating the New Republic capital of Hosnian Prime and its fleet, First Order General Hux aimed his Starkiller weapon at the Resistance base on D'Qar. The Resistance scrambled what few X-wings it had in a desperate attempt to destroy the superweapon's core before it destroyed them. Red and Blue Squadrons fought valiantly in the skies of Starkiller Base while a Resistance team on the ground planted explosives inside the bomb-proof oscillator. The resulting explosion breached the oscillator, permitting Poe to fly into the energy containment system and destroy it with proton torpedoes, sparking the implosion of Starkiller Base.

BEHIND THE SCENES

"I wanted a dragster with a long narrow front and a guy sitting on the back."

—*Star Wars* creator George Lucas on his inspiration for the X-wing

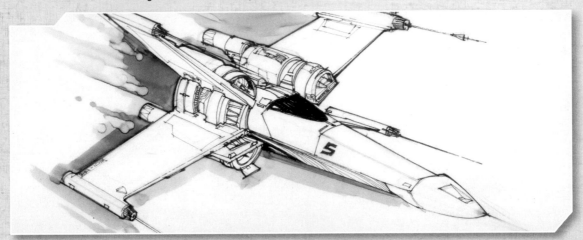

SIX SHOOTER

Colin Cantwell, the *2001: A Space Odyssey* photographic effects specialist George Lucas hired to design the *Star Wars* starships, came up with the idea of opening the wings for the rebel starfighter. He likened the splitting of the S-foils to that of a Western gunslinger drawing his revolver.

ARTISTS' ALLEY

The X-wing was the brainchild of Cantwell and Lucas, but a number of artists contributed to its final design. Joe Johnston revised the starfighter in additional concept sketches, giving it flat canopy windows to minimize reflections during filming. Steve Gawley then made orthographic drawings, adding mechanical details and labeling various components. Finally, Grant McCune and his team at the Industrial Light & Magic (ILM) model shop made practical adjustments, like finding an appropriately shaped snub nose for the ship, during construction of the miniatures.

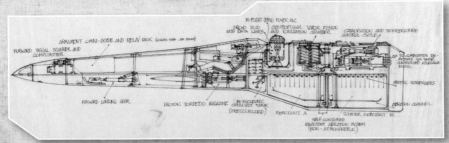

IT'S ELECTRIC!

The X-wing wasn't just any plastic model. The S-foil wings could open and close via a motor. Lightbulbs in each exhaust nacelle created the blue engine glow. Fiber-optic tips allowed the laser cannons to "blink." And to make sure the model didn't burn up, cooling lines of surgical tubing were snaked inside the X-wing's frame.

RED FOR A REASON

George Lucas's screenplay for the initial *Star Wars* film designated the X-wings as "Blue Squadron" and their sister craft, the Y-wings, as "Red Squadron." However, shooting against a blue screen made it impossible for the models to be blue because those parts would blend into the background and disappear on screen. As a consequence, the X-wings had their racing stripes painted red.

PARTS ARE PARTS

Spaceship builders at ILM recycled pieces from model kits for German World War II tanks, Kandy-Vans, Ford Galaxie 500/XLs, and Revell racers to manufacture miniature X-wings and other *Star Wars* starfighters.

FLYBY KNIGHTS

When X-wings flew close to the camera in dogfights with TIE fighters, sound designer Ben Burtt used artillery sounds from the classic movie *The Guns of Navarone* and mixed in a lion's roar or a thunderclap for extra punch and rumble.

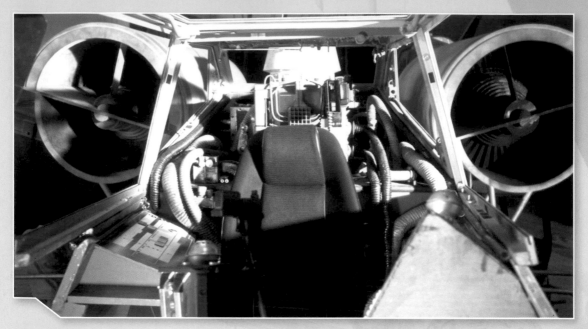

HOT SEAT

All the shots of Luke and the other X-wing pilots were filmed using the same life-size cockpit at Elstree Studios. Former NASA spacecraft designer Harry Lange decorated the set, installing the lights, buttons, switches, and panels to make the console look like that of a real spaceship.

ONLY ONE THERE IS

The original *Star Wars* production budgeted a single, practical X-wing to be built at England's Shepperton Studios, where the throne room and rebel base hangar scenes were shot. Other life-size X-wings were paintings, draped into the shot as backdrops or composited to the film negative during postproduction.

AERIAL ACROBATICS

George Lucas assembled a 16-millimeter reel of film clips featuring World War II fighter planes dipping and weaving around each other to show the aeronautics he envisioned for the Death Star space battle between X-wings and TIE fighters in *Star Wars*.

FRENCH CONNECTIONS

ILM head John Dykstra and his team pioneered motion control techniques and cameras to film the model spaceships. He was determined to make the last reel of *Star Wars* "as exciting as the car chase in *The French Connection*."

BIGGER AND BETTER

For *Return of the Jedi*, model maker Mike Fulmer constructed a "hero version" of the X-wing that, at four feet, was many times larger than the other models. ILM photographed a sweeping flyby close-up of Luke and R2-D2 in the fighter, but the shot was left on the cutting room floor. The model, however, remains a popular attraction in museum tours of *Star Wars* artifacts.

DASHBOARD DREAMS

The Force Awakens production team provided actor Oscar Isaac (Poe Dameron) with a blueprint of his X-wing's console to help make his performance as a starfighter pilot as authentic as possible. It listed the proper steps for a launch sequence, which controls had been used in previous films, and all the new buttons he could press to make up his own flight patterns.

ABOVE: In a single frame, production artist Ralph McQuarrie captures the speed and danger of an X-wing streaking down the confines of the Death Star trench while being harassed by laser fire.

ABOVE: Not yet fully trained in the Force, Luke Skywalker uses a long pole to try to push his starfighter out of the Dagobah bog, to no avail. Production painting by Ralph McQuarrie.

ABOVE: A Resistance X-wing skims over the lakes of Takodana to surprise the First Order forces that have launched a raid on Maz Kanata's castle. Concept art by Kevin Jenkins.

BELOW: The X-wings of the Resistance's Red and Blue Squadrons descend into a vicious swarm of First Order TIE fighters as they attempt to destroy the central oscillator on Starkiller Base. Concept art by James Clyne.

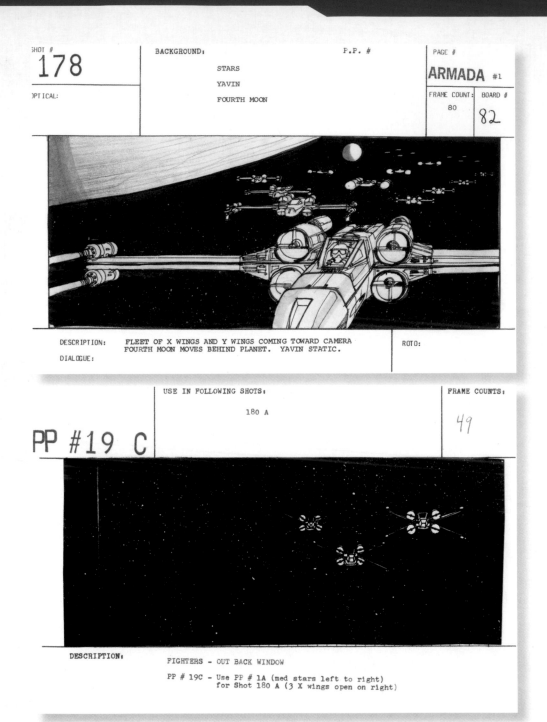

SHOT #

178

OPTICAL:

BACKGROUND:

STARS

YAVIN

FOURTH MOON

P.P. #

PAGE #

ARMADA #1

FRAME COUNT: BOARD #
80   82

DESCRIPTION: FLEET OF X WINGS AND Y WINGS COMING TOWARD CAMERA
FOURTH MOON MOVES BEHIND PLANET.   YAVIN STATIC.

DIALOGUE:

ROTO:

USE IN FOLLOWING SHOTS:

180 A

FRAME COUNTS:

49

PP #19 C

DESCRIPTION: FIGHTERS - OUT BACK WINDOW

PP # 19C - Use PP # 1A (med stars left to right)
for Shot 180 A (3 X wings open on right)

This storyboard sequence provided the miniature effects team with a visual guide for the iconic scene in which the X-wings approach the first Death Star and "lock S-foils in attack position." These heavily detailed drawings ensured that time was not wasted on producing sequences that were not necessary to the film.

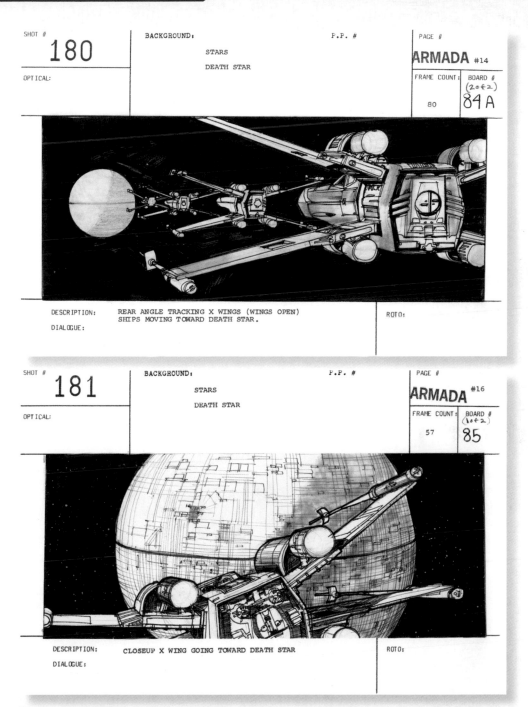

| SHOT # 180 | BACKGROUND: STARS DEATH STAR | P.P. # | PAGE # ARMADA #14 |
| OPTICAL: | | | FRAME COUNT: 80 / BOARD # (20 of 2) 84A |

DESCRIPTION: REAR ANGLE TRACKING X WINGS (WINGS OPEN) SHIPS MOVING TOWARD DEATH STAR.
DIALOGUE:

ROTO:

| SHOT # 181 | BACKGROUND: STARS DEATH STAR | P.P. # | PAGE # ARMADA #16 |
| OPTICAL: | | | FRAME COUNT: 57 / BOARD # (10 of 2) 85 |

DESCRIPTION: CLOSEUP X WING GOING TOWARD DEATH STAR
DIALOGUE:

ROTO:

Since the shots that were filmed often required weeks—if not months—of model-making, motion control photography, and postproduction compositing, preplanning was essential.

INTERVIEW WITH
RICHARD EDLUND

Richard Edlund is one of the pioneers of modern motion picture special effects. He served as the first cameraman for the miniature and optical effects units on *Star Wars* and contributed to the visual and special effects for *The Empire Strikes Back*, *Return of the Jedi*, and *Raiders of the Lost Ark*, all of which won Academy Awards for Edlund and the effects team at Industrial Light & Magic. He founded Boss Film Studios in 1983, where he oversaw the visual and computer effects on films like *Ghostbusters*, *2010: The Year We Make Contact*, and *Air Force One*. He continues to be involved in the industry today, producing his own pictures at Richard Edlund Films.

WHAT FIRST INTERESTED YOU IN SPECIAL EFFECTS?

I went to the USC School of Cinematic Arts when I got out of the Navy. I didn't want to burden my parents, so I decided to get a job. I wound up getting a job with Joe Westheimer. He had an optical house. We did special effects for commercials, TV shows, and a few features. I became a hippie photographer for a couple of years, then got back into the business with Bob Abel. We were doing multipass, very complicated but really beautiful television commercials, like the Butterfly Girl for 7-Up and [also their] "Uncola" campaign.

HOW DID YOU GET INVOLVED IN *STAR WARS*?

I was called by [Industrial Light & Magic head] John Dykstra one day to come out and talk about the possibility of being a cameraman for the *Star Wars* effects unit. Anybody who's in TV wants to do features, and *Star Wars* was a big 20th Century Fox sci-fi movie. I started with a phone and a card table in this huge room in an industrial warehouse building. We had to build the entire photographic system—optical printers, cameras, the motion control equipment, the electronics—from scratch.

WHAT WERE YOUR PRIMARY CONTRIBUTIONS TO *STAR WARS*?

I knew photographic systems backward and forward, I understood the chemistry, I understood the mechanics, optics, and all those kind of things. What I needed to do on *Star Wars* was to design the camera, the camera system, and how we would shoot the miniatures. The boom, the underslung camera, the Trojan helmet moto-point pan-tilt head the camera was situated in, and coming up with ideas to build optical printers—all that stuff was me.

When George came back from shooting in England, I spent about a week with him programming shots, shooting tests, and running the black-and-white tests. I had to teach George how we were going to be able use the system we built. And, like any system, it had limitations.

CAN YOU DESCRIBE THE SYSTEM YOU DEVISED TO SHOOT THE X-WING STARFIGHTERS AND OTHER MINIATURES?

We had twelve channels of motion control, each one of which had to be programmed separately. I had to program the track move, the pan, the tilt, the roll, the swing, the boom, and then the model itself had to be programmed. All of these things had to be done in sequence, because I didn't want to crash the model or crash the camera into the model. I even had a contact mic on the boom so I could hear these various overtones of the motors, which gave me a clue as to how fast I was going with the camera.

HOW DID YOU MANAGE TO SHOOT MULTIPLE X-WINGS IN ONE SHOT?

The thing is, in *Star Wars* we had so many elements to shoot—there were thousands of elements involved in putting in the compositing. And most of the X-wings were shot separately. I would run a shot of an X-wing through the Moviola film editor with the take of the next X-wing that was supposed to be in the shot. I would bipack [combine] those in the Moviola and see how they worked together. Once I did the first test and it looked good, I'd shoot the beauty pass of the X-wing against blue screen. Then I had to break that setup down.

WHAT WERE SOME CHALLENGES YOU FACED WHILE FILMING THE CLIMACTIC DEATH STAR TRENCH BATTLE?

We discovered that in running the camera down the trench, the camera could only shoot the first forty feet of it. I had to figure out how to use forced perspective paintings at the end of the trench. I'd line the shots up so that I could do three runs down the trench with the camera and then seamlessly join the other two shots, the end of one to the beginning of the next. Sometimes we'd have to project things through the camera to line them up. It was a lot of seat-of-the-pants work. You'd have to do a test and see how it worked. If you got it almost right, you tweaked it a little bit and you got it better, and then you go for it, you shoot it.

DID SOME OF THE X-WING MODELS SUFFER BATTLE DAMAGE OF THEIR OWN?

In order to get the dynamics of the movie that George needed, I was virtually scraping the model with the camera. Sometimes I'd break the tip off an X-wing's laser and have to call the model shop to come out and fix it!

MAKE IT YOUR OWN

One of the great things about IncrediBuilds models is that each one is completely customizable. The untreated natural wood can be decorated with paints, pencils, pens—the list goes on and on!

Before you start building and decorating your model, read through the included instruction sheet so you understand how all the pieces come together. Then, choose a theme and make a plan. Do you want to make an exact replica of an X-wing or create something completely wacky? The choice is yours! Here are some sample projects to get those creative juices flowing.

Every X-wing has its own droid.
You can make these any color you like.

For a simple stand, paint it black. Then use a
silver permanent marker to outline the base.

T-65B X-WING

Re-create the iconic starfighter that carrie the rebels to victory over the Death Star in *New Hope*. When making a replica, it's alwa good to study an actual image of what you are trying to copy. Look closely at the detai found in this book and brainstorm how you can re-create them.

WHAT YOU NEED
- Matte white acrylic paint
- Yellow, gray, blue, and red paint
- Pencil
- Gray chalk pastel
- Cotton swab

WHAT YOU MIGHT WANT
- Piece of sandpaper
- Detail brush (18/0 size or smaller)
- Silver permanent marker

1. Assemble the model, but leave the wings, laser cannons, and stand off.
2. Paint the assembled model white.
3. Separately, paint the wings and laser cannons white.
4. Add coats of paint as needed. **TIP: Use sandpaper in between coats of paint for a smoother finish.**
5. Once the pieces are dry, paint the yellow details onto the main model, the wings, and the laser cannons. Let dry.
6. Paint the back of the engines and the deflector shield generator gray. Then add the gray details to the wings. **TIP: To create a gradient (from dark to light), use a graphite pencil for the shading.**

7. Paint the red stripe on both sides of the ship.
8. Add the red details to the wings. The red stripes at the top of the wings are the call sign for the ship. You can add more or fewer stripes to denote different X-wings. Five red stripes make it Luke Skywalker's. This example is Red Four, piloted by John D. Branon during the battle of Yavin.
9. Assemble the model.
10. To finish, rub chalk pastel—using a cotton swab—around the ship to add some weathering.

CRASH LANDING!

On a mission to find Master Yoda, Luke Skywalker and R2-D2 find their X-wing sinking beneath the swamps of Dagobah. Yoda masterfully uses his knowledge of the Force to retrieve the X-wing for them. Re-create the X-wing that emerges from the swamp in *The Empire Strikes Back* with this project.

WHAT YOU NEED

- White, yellow, gray, red, black, brown, and green paint
- Paintbrush

WHAT YOU MIGHT WANT

- Detail brush (18/0 size or smaller)
- Two or more shades of green paint
- Two or more shades of brown paint
- White colored pencil
- Red colored pencil
- Light blue paint

TIP:
Adding black or white to a color will change its shade.

Start by creating a replica X-wing using steps 1 through 10 of the T-65B X-wing instructions. Remember to add five stripes of red to indicate that this is Luke Skywalker's X-wing.

Using the brown paint, start dabbing "dirt" onto the X-wing. Use your paintbrush to blend it in with the background color until you get the effect you want. If you have more than two shades of brown, start with the darker brown and use the lighter shade next.

Add the swampy greenery. Using dark green paint, paint green lines that drape around the ship. Go back and add rounded leaf shapes to those lines. To get more depth, go back and add lighter green to some.

Repeat steps 2 and 3 until you like how swampy it looks.

FOR A DIFFERENT EFFECT, color the pieces with white colored pencil before you assemble. Add the red stripe in colored pencil as well. You will paint over them next, but the pencil underneath creates more texture. It will also require fewer coats of paint!

THE SWAMPY STAND:

1. Paint the stand gray. Don't let the paint dry.

2. Wet your paintbrush and use light blue paint to create a wash over the gray stand.

3. Wiggle your paintbrush from the center of the stand toward the edge to create ripples.

4. Add more white to the top of the stand for fog. Blend well with the existing gray.

5. Use a small paintbrush to paint a green outline around the stand. The line shouldn't be neat and straight. Instead paint more rounded shapes to give the look of trees and bushes.

SOURCES

Blackman, Haden. *Star Wars: The New Essential Guide to Vehicles and Vessels*. New York: Del Rey, 2003.

Bray, Adam, Cole Horton, Kerrie Dougherty, and Michael Kogge. *Star Wars: Absolutely Everything You Need to Know*. New York: Dorling Kindersley, 2015.

Bouzerau, Laurent. *Star Wars: The Annotated Screenplays*. New York: Del Rey, 1997.

Dougherty, Kerrie, Hans Jessen, Curtis Saxton, David West Reynolds, and Ryder Windham. *Star Wars: Complete Vehicles*. New York: Dorling Kindersley, 2013.

Fry, Jason. *Star Wars: The Force Awakens Incredible Cross-Sections*. New York: Dorling Kindersley, 2015.

Hidalgo, Pablo. *Star Wars: The Force Awakens: The Visual Dictionary*. New York: Dorling Kindersley, 2015.

Murphy, Paul. *Star Wars: The Rebel Alliance Sourcebook*. Honesdale, PA: West End Games, 1990.

Peterson, Lorne. *Sculpting a Galaxy*. San Rafael, CA: Insight Editions, 2006.

Rinzler, J.W. *The Making of Star Wars: The Definitive Story Behind the Original Film*. New York: Del Rey, 2007.

———. *The Sounds of Star Wars*. San Francisco: Chronicle, 2010.

———. *Star Wars: The Blueprints*. Seattle: 47North, 2013.

Slavicsek, Bill and Curtis Smith. *The Star Wars Sourcebook*. Honesdale, PA: West End Games, 1987.

Smith, Bill. *Star Wars: The Essential Guide to Vehicles and Vessels*. New York: Del Rey, 1996.

Windham, Ryder. *Star Wars: Millennium Falcon Owner's Workshop Manual*. New York: Del Rey, 2011.

ABOUT THE AUTHOR

MICHAEL KOGGE's other recent work includes *Empire of the Wolf*, an epic graphic novel about werewolves in ancient Rome and the junior novels for *Batman v Superman* and *Star Wars: The Force Awakens*, along with the *Star Wars Rebels* series of books. He resides online at www.MichaelKogge.com, while his real home is located in Southern California.

IncrediBuilds™
A Division of Insight Editions LP
PO Box 3088
San Rafael, CA 94912
www.insighteditions.com

Find us on Facebook: www.facebook.com/InsightEditions
Follow us on Twitter: @insighteditions

Library of Congress Cataloging-in-Publication Data available.

ISBN: 978-1-68298-011-8

Publisher: Raoul Goff
Acquisitions Manager: Robbie Schmidt
Art Director: Chrissy Kwasnik
Designer: Edwin Kuo
Executive Editor: Vanessa Lopez
Managing Editor: Molly Glover
Senior Editor: Chris Prince
Production Editor: Elaine Ou
Associate Editor: Katie DeSandro
Production Manager: Thomas Chung
Production Coordinator: Sam Taylor
Craft and Instruction Development: Rebekah Piatte
Model Design: Ryan Zhang and Ball Cheung, Team Green

Insight Editions would like to thank Curt Baker, Leland Chee, Pablo Hidalgo, Samantha Holland, Daniel Saeva, and Krista Wong.

ROOTS of PEACE   REPLANTED PAPER

Insight Editions, in association with Roots of Peace, will plant two trees for each tree used in the manufacturing of this book. Roots of Peace is an internationally renowned humanitarian organization dedicated to eradicating land mines worldwide and converting war-torn lands into productive farms and wildlife habitats. Roots of Peace will plant two million fruit and nut trees in Afghanistan and provide farmers there with the skills and support necessary for sustainable land use.

Manufactured in China by Insight Editions

10 9 8 7 6 5 4